Annie

DENNIS OF PENGE

For all the Wendys; may you find your Dennis.
And for Susan, who helped me find mine.

In memory of Nitsa, long-term resident of Brookhurst Court,
auntie, survivor, hilarious, sass to spare.
Miss you hard.

OBERON BOOKS
LONDON

WWW.OBERONBOOKS.COM

First published in 2018 by Oberon Books Ltd
521 Caledonian Road, London N7 9RH
Tel: +44 (0) 20 7607 3637 / Fax: +44 (0) 20 7607 3629
e-mail: info@oberonbooks.com
www.oberonbooks.com

A catalogue record for this book is available from the British Library.

PB ISBN: 9781786826763
E ISBN: 9781786826756

Cover image: Jon Attfield

Printed and bound by 4EDGE Limited, Hockley, Essex, UK.
eBook conversion by Lapiz Digital Services, India.

10 9 8 7 6 5 4 3 2 1

Foreword

I n early 2016 I got sober, and in order to help my sobriety, started writing articles for a sobriety website. I noticed that all the other articles seemed to paint an entirely positive picture of sobriety. (My skin is so glowing! I have so much energy! I look so young! I've lost so much weight!) There are obvious, benevolent reasons for that – encouragement, for instance – but it seemed like a half-truth and it felt really important to share the difficulties as well as the positives with other early sober people. For me, one of the hardest things about early sobriety was the debilitating and medievally demonic depression that overtook me for the first six months, which everyone in the literature seemed to be keeping a secret.

Later this was replaced by the strain of not feeling the release and disinhibition of substances – of never being OUT OF MY HEAD – and having to retrain myself to feel those things without them. It seemed like such hard, tedious work. It seemed that in the sobriety literature, no one was talking about this either. So I started writing about looking for Dionysus – the god of transcendence and ecstasy – who I anglicised as Dennis – in various experiences I made myself undertake. At the same time I read Johann Hari's book on addiction, *Chasing the Scream*, which controversially and convincingly posits that addiction is not in fact a progressive disease but a symptom of a lack of connection. I'd also been obsessed by Target Culture and its nefarious influence on our whole social structure and sense of ourselves since watching Adam Curtis's *The Trap*, and seeing and experiencing its inhumane results in the mental health and benefits system at first hand; I wanted to ask what happens to people in the system when they are deemed well enough to leave it – but without a structure or community to support them. An unrepentant Londoner by birth and choice, I wrote an ode to London in my last show, *How (Not) to Live in Suburbia*, and in this show I focus in on my childhood ends of Penge, one of the last ungentrified places in London, but rapidly changing.

My last show was unabashedly autobiographical, and this time I wanted to create an epic, mythical, heroic tale without me in it. Wendy and Hortense are real people from my childhood and Dennis is also based on a composite of childhood friends, so there is a lot of me in this show, but it's not about me.

I've always been obsessed by the Bacchae, how economically and devastatingly it tells the truth, and right now it feels like we need this tale of opposing societal/psychic forces more than ever. So I've borrowed heavily and unapologetically from Euripides in the structure and form of *Dennis*.

The making of this show has been an interesting one (and not without complexities). I'd like to shout out to my oaken hearted producers, Jen and Emma, for being absolute legends. I'd like to raise a glass of zero per cent beer to Alex Rogerson, our Arts Council relationship manager. I'd like to ululate to the whole team, who are solid gold mensches, and to everyone at the venues who has supported this project on its sometimes bumpy road from its inception through to now. You are noticed. We massively appreciate you.

I've made this show with a brilliant composer, Asaf Zohar. It's our first collaboration and his first theatre piece and I'm extremely excited about it. We'd like you to be able to listen to the music Asaf has written so if you contact the company we can provide you with a download code in due course.

Hope you enjoy.

Annie Siddons, August 2018.

Dennis of Penge opened at Ovalhouse, London, on 27th September 2018, then transferred to The Albany Deptford on 6th October.

Writer	Annie Siddons
Composer	Asaf Zohar
Director	Laura Keefe
Direction of R and D processes	Justin Audibert
Performers	Jorell Coiffic-Kamall, Annie Siddons, Asaf Zohar
Sound design	Mike Winship
Technical Stage Manager	Aime Neeme
Lighting Design	Andy Purves
Producer	Jen Smethurst
Strategic Producer	Emma Bettridge
Assistant Director	David Gilbert
Movement Consultant	Dan Cunningham
Costume	Melanie Brooks
Cover Image	Jon Attfield

With love and thanks to Owen, Stella, Sam and everyone at Ovalhouse, Linda and all at The Albany, Brian and CPT family for early support, Nicki Hobday for early input, Craig Stein for early development, Charlotte Bennett for early input, George Easterbrook for sterling work, Reena at Battersea Arts Centre for early encouragement, Emma and Bristol Ferment for early support. Co-commissioned by Ovalhouse and The Albany Deptford, with support from Battersea Arts Centre. Funded by Arts Council of England.

"To affirm the Dionysian is to recognise the play of pain and death in life and to tolerate the full range from death to life and pain to ecstasy"

Tom Moore

"Human beings only become addicted when they cannot find any-thing better to live for and when they desperately need to fill the emptiness that threatens to destroy them"

Bruce Alexander,
Inventor of the Rat Park Addiction Experiment

"If you imagine someone who is brave enough to withdraw all his projections, then you get an individual who is conscious of a pretty thick shadow. Such a man has saddled himself with new problems and conflicts. He has become a serious problem to him-self, as he is now unable to say that they do this or that, they are wrong, and they must be fought against... Such a man knows that whatever is wrong in the world is in himself, and if he on-ly learns to deal with his own shadow he has done something real for the world. He has succeeded in shouldering at least an in-finitesimal part of the gigantic, unsolved social problems of our day."

C J Jung

"I realise what I said at some times may have over-emphasised rationality, Human beings are much more complicated than the human being as a businessman. Only two groups of people behave rationally at all times. Economists and psychopaths."

John Nash,
Creator of Game Theory, progenitor of target culture.

Note on Performance.

We divided up the text in rehearsals according to our skills and proclivities. Asaf played nearly all the music, with support from me and Jorell. You can do the whole thing as a solo performance with a band and choir or divide it up between thirty people. It's all good. To get hold of our original score, please contact us.

1. Prologue

CHORUS:

> Sometimes you need a god to come from the east
> And tear shit up.
> Sometimes enough is enough.
> Sometimes you need someone with an overview.
> Sometimes we call, and are heard.
> Do you hear the bees?
> They're buzzing; take heed.
> Ronnie and Johnny did for us.
> They didn't MEAN to.
> They were just trying to rebalance
> The old elitisms;
> The folderol and the flimflam.
> But it's all gone too far,
> and we're dying
> now. The ghosts are keening.
> Arm yourselves.

2. Chicken Sermon

> *{Co-performer vocalises Gospel vocals through this.]*
> South London. The tube don't come here,

but it's alright –

there's chicken.

Chicken is the opium of the people!

Chicken is the staple of the people!

Chicken is our bread and butter!

Chicken is our alpha and omega!

We eat so much chicken we

ARE chicken!

We eat so much chicken, the pavements are High with Bones!

And the Dogs

Are Superstrong Wolfdogs, fanged and ready.

We are protein, rich and breadcrumbed.

We Eat Fantastic Melly's Chicken!

Thirty-five branches from Addington to Peckham.

(Melly's curly font has its imitators

But everybody in the ends knows who is the originator.)

Fantastic Melly's Chicken is ambitious.

Don't think about welfare, just enjoy it's delicious

grease and spice and deep, deep comfort.

As your girth expands and your arteries contract,

Your Soul exalts.

As you bite into the Crispy Brown Fist of meat,

Don't think about which bit of the bird you eat!

Sometimes the fries are perfect and golden.

and sometimes they are pale and frozen.

The sauce is generic – but two quid with pop! Mate –

Everybody's down at the chicken shop!

Everybody's down at the chicken shop!

No matter how shit your day has been,

No matter how low the world wants to make you,

No matter if the money came from the back of the sofa,

No matter if no one respects you,

No matter if you haven't been touched in a sex way for a while,

No matter if your ideas go unheard,

(Or even unspoken because you're shy)

Fantastic Melly's Chicken is a church that welcomes all,

salves all, in its battery, delicious, opiate, salty wings.

It's cross, the fluorescent perky cock's face:

You see it, you know you're welcome and will find solace.

You won't be judged.

You will be redeemed,

By the Holy Trinity of Wings, Fries and Coke

Ready to face the next bit of the shit

That life spits.

You're a small god.

3. Introducing Wendy

Into the SE20 branch of FMC (that's Fantastic Melly's Chicken to you and me)

Rolls Wendy. Heroine of this story.

She's had a time of it. (We'll go back and detail it shortly.)

In fact, she's hit rock bottom.

Her new rock bottom,

Below where everyone thought the bottom was,

Below the deep deep abyss

With the soul's angler fish,

Each one just laughing at her fall in terms of how low a soul can go

And still be a soul,
so low; solo.
In FMC the mood is joke.
Kids are listening to Capital Reloaded,
Singing along to old school Craig David.
Wendy orders. Wings, fries, and a coke.
She's morbidly obese, dressed for comfort –
Her goal is just to shuffle back to her flat,
Lick her fingers,
And cross off another day.
She hands over her two quid, coppers and lint.
The guy serving her has a glint
in his green green eye. His fingers touch hers.
She jolts.
In his hand her chubby fingers he enfolds:
Her skin is pallid and his is gold.
He makes her meet his gaze.
Wendy! he says Oh my days!
Wendy! My queen!
Who the fuck is this, she says –
There's a thrill of recognition in her chubby hand,
Some kaleidoscopic shift of memory and love/stab/pang
Holds her still there, her hand in his hand:
She's not waiting for her change.
She's going to a distant land.

4. 1992.

[Co-performer vocalises Aladdin 'I Can Show You the World' through this.]

1992. She's ten, wiry, pyjama-ed, sitting in Hortense's flat

Felt tips all over the floor,

drawing imaginary worlds.

Her cheap knock-off pyjamas

have some kind of aspirational girl figure on them.

Some kind of wonky Princess imitation Jasmine.

Low production values, cheap ink.

Everyone knows

Jasmine's outfit should be sea green

But it's dirty yellow. The wrongness is blatant.

But Wendy loves these jams. In them she feels safe,

And next to her is her one true friend.

His name is Dennis.

He's drawing mythical figures with dextrous fingers,

And claiming they're real:

A woman dying from a lightning bolt,

And a man with a baby in his thigh.

Those are my parents, he says:

No one's ever seen who Dennis' parents are, so why not?

Hortense brings cocoa and Turkish biscuits

Dennis eats seventeen at once.

And they're singing

"I can show you the world

Shining, na na na splendid!"

They only saw the film one time.

It's not out on VHS yet,

But the song is seared on their hearts,
And it's true. From the window of the flat,
On the 14th floor of an estate that is called
Elysium Fields,
Wendy and Dennis can see the world,
And Wendy is happy.

5. Now.

"MOVE, FAT BITCH!"
The next one in line: He's starving, he's busy,
ain't got time to consider that Wendy
is a person with pride and dignity.
She's snapped out of her reverie
And back in to the present.
The man pushes her.
He seems to resent her very existence.

Excuse me, says the green eyed Dennis,
For it is he –
Twenty-five years apart and it's unmistakably him –
I'm serving this Queen,
Wait your turn man.
The man kisses his teeth at Dennis,
And Dennis just looks at him,
And the man stops spitting his sentence.
I'm serving this Queen,
Wait your turn, man.
Dennis! Is that you?
Yeh Wendy, it's me.

How the fuck you been?

6. Wendy's head

How can Wendy tell Dennis that she is not okay,
That she'd been thinking maybe of ending it today?
That – twenty-five years since she last saw him
Her hopes and dreams have got so thin
That one foot in front of the other takes all that she's got,
And that making it to the chicken shop
Is like climbing fucking Everest's Peak.
She's sober now, but her heart is bleak.
He doesn't even know. It's been twenty-five years.
Wendy finds herself sobbing fat tears –
Nah, man – not cool, not here, not now
She ducks out. He calls out.
Wendy!
Wendy!
What's up?
Wendy!
Quick vault over the counter
And Dennis has found her.
Her slow shuffle, her old lady kicks,
Accidental normcore, brandless.
She needs a shower, she smells sick
But Dennis holds her in his caress.
Whatever's going on, we can fix – I'm here.
Nothing can go wrong when I am near.
Wendy and Dennis like the old days
Tearing it up – what do you say?

Wendy's face is pure pain.
To see this boy she loves again
Explodes her heart into tiny bits.
Fuck you, Dennis, she vehemently spits,
You're thirty-five, working in fast food,
Like selling chicken to losers is cool –
It's sad. All those kids think you're tragic
– no one thinks you got no magic,
Not even me. But Dennis just smiles.
I got plans for us Wend,
I'll tell you next time you swing by.
And with that, he kisses his friend,
Revaults the counter, and sings,
As he sells his two quid fries and wings.

7. Shad Thames.

Shad Thames.
1982 was the time between Bohemia and Conranisation.
Hortense Honeysett, legal secretary, first generation,
Jamaican,
Liked to walk there.
She liked the stink of it,
And its evocations.
After work the lost spiciness could be smelt on the breeze,
And the lost artistry.
She was still young then,
But her heart was locked tight.
No man could thaw her
Except Jesus.

Dainty Hortense, her T Bar brown patent shoes and her
tan tights

Her tight muscles and her brown skirt,

Her brown handbag, shiny,

Her faux pearls and her pink knits,

Her high butt and her high tits,

Her high mind, wishing she could study the law,

Walking after work to wash out

the stink of work and replace it with

the stink of sanctity.

In 1982 she is thirty-eight years old.

Walking by the fetid Thames one day,

she's thinking of this verse from Revelations:

"Then the angel showed me the river of the water of life,
bright as

Crystal, flowing from the throne of

God and of the Lamb, through the middle of the street of
the City"

And as if the river were playing along

with her biblical bent,

This is what it sent.

A thin ugly baby, pink and blotchy,

a low-rent female Moses

in a chicken-in-a-basket-basket.

Proper foundling,

Proper foul,

In a fowl basket,

A spewed up gift from the riverine gods –

And Hortense, not even thinking,

Clasped this maggoty baby to her chest

9

wrapped her worn brown coat around her –
And took her on the train to Penge West.
And this was Wendy.

8. Wendy and Hortense Song

For ten years
Hortense loves Wendy hard,
and she won't admit, even to herself,
that Wendy is lacking in any regard,
And every day she says to Wendy
You are enough Wendy
and so despite Wendy being quick to hurt and cry,
and slow to learn and to defend herself,
She's okay. She can move, and her smile is captivating
and she has a friend,
the boy called Dennis,
some light brown foreigner,
(No idea where he sprung from.)
And Hortense says *you know what girl?*
You are enough.
and Wendy feels like she's enough, feels loved with the
deep love.
In turn Wendy knows that she loves Hortense
Loves to cuddle her and smell her scent
Loves her upright and queenly
But also in her Winceyette nightie
Loves the inflections of her voice
Which seems every year to get more Jamaican
resisting the twang of Londonisation
Loves that she is there every day

Loves her rare laughter
Her smiles precious as hummingbirds
The longed for eye creases that mean Hortense is merry.
She also plays her, resisting her strictness
Needing to kick down the propriety
In order to inhabit it more graciously
So they clash sometimes
And Hortense sometimes slaps Wendy's scrawny behind
But Wendy always knows Hortense is kind.
Wendy always knows Hortense is ki-

9. Wendy

Now, back at her multiple occupancy private flat
Twenty men and her
One bathroom
Individual electric meters
One kitchen that she never goes into
cos squalor cos shyness
Memories – unbidden – flood Wendy.
The emotional Bends.
She's tried to lock this shit up tight
But seeing Dennis has disturbed the sedimentary layers
And now she can't stop reliving
What happened the morning after the Aladdin sleepover
When she last saw him.

10. 1992

The next morning
When Dennis left
Wendy'd kicked off
Refused to get dressed.
And made Hortense late.
And Hortense didn't do late,
She was immaculate.
So now she's running out the door for the last possible safe train.
In the t-bar shoes she still favours, she's clip clip clipping,
as fast as she can,
Till she encounters a binbag dripping.
And now suddenly she's slip slip slipping, Hortense,
She slips in one moment and in the next she slips again
and then she trips on the greasy drips, and this third
slip catapults her from the top
of the Elysium Fields –
Fa doom fa doom, fa doom, head over her patent heels.

Fa doom fa doom
Down two flights of stairs.

Fa doom, Fa doom,fa doom Fa doom Fa doom
Down another five flights of stairs
and all her kindness all her wisdom
all her probity all her gravity all her dignity all her
absolute QUEEN to the DOM
cannot prevent her body from reacting predictably
to the force and the violence of the tumble.

She ends, Hortense,

Right there and then.

The legal secretary

And surrogate mother to Wendy

The woman of intelligence and integrity

Of ferocity and beauty

Of a mind full of knowledge and yearning

Of religion and book learning

And untapped potential

She just lies there, bones

bent back like mistakes

Blood from her mouth and head

And her dark eyes so dead

Maybe she ends up in the real

Elysian Fields

It would be good wouldn't it

In the arms of the original honeyed boy, Jesus.

She deserves it

A quiet life of love lived without

pomp

Or grandiosity

deserving some reward beyond the memory of the one person who

loves her back.

Wendy.

11. Now. Wendy.

Understandably, Wendy can't get to sleep after this. Sleep doesn't even bother laughing at her: it just shrugs like –
Nah. Not you. til it gets bored, and when it gets bored,

the rosy fingers of the dawn are already teasing the night into rolling over on its belly, **you win.**

And when Wendy does sleep, her dreams are more horror than her waking.

A slow mo replay of watching Hortense's neighbour Dawn taking out her bins, and the **drip drip drip** of Melly's chicken grease,beer,and other unidentifiable substances, across the hall and down the stairs. Banal. Fatal.

She wakes sweat soaked at one, her mouth foul with horror.

And her first realisation on waking is that she has to deal with Neil.

12. Neil Pratt.

Let's talk about Neil PRATT.

Neil Pratt. Bullying survivor, thirty-eight, now makes his money out of questionnaires. Decision Maker for *"PENTHEUS Care Consortium"* – a private company that aims to act as a *"one stop shop"* for all the unloved – his role is to assign numbers to suffering, and crunch them. Exceeding targets gives him a semi – and is fiscally rewarded. Creating a hostile environment for the sick makes his sphincter tingle – and tops up his pension plan. He excels at it and has been "fast tracked". This pleases him. This pleases his wife, Melanie. This has bought him a different kind of semi in Bromley, 1930s, alarms for intruders.

In Wendy's Work Capability Assessment, after she'd accidentally burned her flat down when off her tits, after prison, six months into substance recovery, (diagnosed with Borderline Personality Disorder, Learning Difficulties, Autism Spectrum Disorder, Bipolar Disorder 1, PTSD, and long-term substance dependency, if you're asking –) Neil added a jaunty question based on his own private after dinner reading.

What Colour is your Parachute Wendy?

You what?

What transferable skills do you have?

What?

What are you good at?

Wendy could just remember at that time that she had loved to draw, had loved to dance.

I like drawing.

I like dancing.

There's no category for that Wendy. This isn't a talent agency. HA!

There are so many more questions that day, intrusive, baroque, just fucking weird.

This was one: *on a scale of one to ten, how many showers would you say you've had in the past week?*

What do you mean, on a scale of one to ten? That don't even make no sense. Do you mean have I had ten showers or one?

From the evidence, I'd say not more than one.

From the evidence, says Wendy with her eyes, I'd say you're a cunt.

With her mouth, she says nothing.

14. Neil Pratt

Today Neil has called her in to discuss an appointment that she has apparently missed. She still hasn't had the result of her Work Capability Assessment.

Her appointment is at 2.30 and it's 1.15 and she's full of Hortense.

Events that occur.

1. At 1.15 – no wash/ no breakfast – Wendy shuffles down to the bus stop. The 197 is diverted. Gasworks. It's gonna take her an extra forty-five MINUTES to get there. Croydon, the Mecca.

Wendy grapples with the forced memory of Hortense's landing. Swastika shaped.

2. On the 197, there's beef between two kids over the terminology used in a snapchat burn and the driver – Rasta, supreme emotional intelligence that doesn't translate into his pay grade – stops the bus to make the kids learn a lesson, with lightly worn gravitas.

Swastikas dance along the insides of Wendy's eyelids. She wants to scratch out her eyes.

3. The sun is caressing the jaunty font that adorns the front of the PENTHEUS building. It's a kind of bastardised comic sans, grossly upbeat, it's can-do attitude and perky welcome in direct opposition to the misery the PENTHEANS mete out.

Fadoom Fadoom Fadoom Fadoom

4. Wendy forces herself to break into a run. It's not good. Her body doesn't understand. It's been years. In her body, in her head, in her soul, is Hortense. She arrives, flushed, stinking, sweat-soaked and ten minutes late.

For her ten minutes of lateness, they will make her wait three hours and seventeen minutes. She pulls the number out of the number thing and they bypass it, time and again and time and time again.

It's like her sweaty fat body is creating a scent memory because all she can smell is Lily of the Valley, Hortense's scent.

– *Wendy Honeysett. You were late.*

– I'm sorry, I.

– *You're not making good choices Wendy.*

– I don't know what this appointment is for.

– *Now Wendy you missed our CV enhancement training day and I've got to say I have to sanction your jobseeker's benefit.*

– I'm not on jobseeker's though! I never got no letter! Wendy holds her voice steady, tries to not whine, she feels like a naughty toddler not understanding that you can't smear shit on walls.

– *Not according to this.*

– What?

– *Failed Work Capability Assessment. Put on Jobseekers'. Failed to turn up for CV enhancement training day. Failed to appeal against rejected WCA. If you want to, you can apply for the hardship fund using form JSA/ESA1QJP whilst you apply for the appeal and you can also reapply for JSA but you will need to attend WRA's whenever we say and you can also contact the HAAAS.*

– I don't understand a single thing you just said to me. Your mouth moves but it's just wahmwahmwahmwahmwahmwahnumbernumbernumber

– *Don't take that tone. I can give you the food bank details. I can give you the form JSA/ESA1QJP.*

– I'm waiting for a decision from the "Decision Maker". I never got no letter.

– *The form JSA/ESA1QJP you can find over there. If you get it you will get 43.85 a week. You were deemed fit for work, you know that Wendy.*

– No, I never got no letter.

– *You were called in for an appointment. And yet you still couldn't make the effort to be here on time?*

– It's not about effort. Effort is what your wife has to do to ride you, smallcock wasteman!

– *Your attitude is disrespectful. Security!*

– Your attitude is one of a total cunt, says Wendy with
her eyes, and with her mouth she says nothing, kisses her
teeth, leaves in the arms of Barry and Stu, security guards,
just doing their job, nothing personal.

———————————————————

14 Wendy and Dennis

Two and a half hours later, Wendy arrives back at her flat.
Spatchcocked.

Crumples onto her mattress, sleeps again.

In her sweaty hunger fuelled dreams, there are drawings,
there is Hortense, there is Dennis.

I got plans for us Wend. I'll tell you next time you swing
by.

The uphill shuffle to the chicken shop takes longer today.

She doesn't have two quid, only 1.43, and some foreign
currency that the kid in the newsagent gave her as change
when she was too glassy with pain to realise.

Nonetheless. She's impelled.

You came back, he says, and smiles,

gold tooth at the corner,

he's so good looking.

What happened to Wendy's libido in the years of fuckery
was, it got parked.

And now it stirs.

He's so good looking, he must be a chichiman, thinks
Wendy.

Why didn't I know this before.

———————————————————————

Wendy doggedly lays into the Family Treat Combo
Dennis has presented her with/ She is so hungry her
hunger is hungry/ She is so hungry her stomach isn't even
growling any more, it's just sulking/ The spice on the
wings the grease on the fries the fizz of the coke/ Not as
good as the other coke obvs but her dopamine is hit/ ping
ping ping. Momentarily Hortense fades, blowing a kiss.

How was your day?

It was shit. There's this guy at Pentheus. I hate him. They
cut my money. He don't listen.

Do you still have any of our pictures Wend?

The ones we used to draw

Back in the day?

What are you talking about?

I know you kept them!

I never used to draw.

Find them Wend! Bring me them pictures!

What have you got to lose?

Nothing.

I got NOTHING to lose.

Exactly!

I'm sober.

I know.

How do you know?

I have my ways!

What stalking me now is it, that's sketchy af!

I'm not stalking you.

I just KNOW YOU Wend.

You don't know me! You left me!

I got plans for us. Say, in a few weeks. You ready for my
big Dennis Plans?

I don't go out after dark, kids, dogs, I'm scared.

You can be queen of the night with me.

Go fuck some next chick Dennis stop taking the piss.

You're my queen, Wendy.

Take my hand. Do you trust me?

No.

----

15. Dennis and Neil

Bromley, 7.30. There is a knock at the door.

Melanie Pratt looks up from the Jamie Oliver seafood lasagne she is making.

Neil! Neil! Door babes!

Neil, slightly resentful that he has to open the door WHEN HE HAS ONLY JUST GOT BACK FROM WORK, does so.

A beautiful man is standing there.

Hello Neil.

Do I know you?

I'm a friend of one of your clients

You can't come to my house!

The man smiles and Neil feels strange feelings inside himself.

The man smells slightly of fried chicken but carries himself like a King. Neil is confused.

I'm Dennis. I'm here from my friend Wendy Honeysett. I just wanted to ask you…

Neil loses his words, puffs out his chest. Recovering he says

You can't come here to my house and ask me questions.
You have an issue, go through the proper channels.

I do have an issue, says Dennis, smiling steadily.

My friend – Wendy Honeysett – was very upset today at
the way she's been treated. And I have to say, to me, it
sounded somewhat disrespectful.

I'm not discussing this with you, Neil thinks he says.

Actually he says – *she stinks, your friend, she's always late,
she's rude and ignorant, she swears, she shouts, she cries,
she's surly she has never once smiled at me, she's an addict,
unemployable, poor social skills, FAT!*

Quietly Dennis says – you don't allow people to be divine,
you define them with numbers from 0-9. Expecting their
divinity when you won't allow them a chance to feel the
infinite godliness inside themselves? Punishing poverty
with poverty? Labelling? Shaming? Does that work? Tell
me, bruv. I'm curious.

Don't bruv me!

Okay. Have it your way.

Dennis turns away, is gone.

————————————————

Neil tries to shut the door with all the fury and pomp that
he feels.

And at this point the ivy that covers the fences of
Neil's next door neighbours, the Khans, shucks itself
languorously off the fence and starts to move.

Across the patio it snakes and tendrils

There is so much of it

It's coming for Neil

A leafy boa

He is transfixed

Watching it come

coiling and snaking

It comes for him, purposefully

He can't move

Round his ankles

round his knees

round his thighs

Across his belly

towards his genitals.

It starts to snake around his throat, his nostrils, his eyes.

He is terrified!

He is also having a mild anaphylactic reaction.

Melanie finds him there an hour later,

Wrapped up like a pupa.

Motionless

The police are poker faced and respectful.

Take down a description of the poultry magician.

The lasagne is delicious, particularly good clams,

But Neil is shaken from head to toe.

Can't enjoy it.

Can't sleep.

Cellulosy, Chlorophylly.

Tendrils coming through his throat,

winding around his bronchioles,

Squeezing his aorta.

Has dreams of leafy asphyxiation.

16. Chorus

Buzz Buzz
Bzzzzzzzz Bzzzzzzz
Can you hear them bees
Unseasonal bees
Delusional bees
They're calling
They're warning
A new day is dawning
Nectar-fat
Plump-drunk
Clumsy-dopy
The bees of Zagreus
Buzz Buzz Buzz.
Don't worry Persephone
He will rescue you from the freeze
Don't worry Persephone
He will thaw you put you at your ease
You called and he heard
His godliness stirred
The paradigm shifts
The horror lifts
All the ghosts are rising
Wait. If it was that simple,
we'd all be free already.

17. Day One Post Ivygate

Day one post Ivygate, it's time for Neil to clap-back.

Discombobulated by his Dennis encounter,

He wakes the next morning in a foul mood.

Can't clear his throat.

Little tiny ivy hairs stuck in it.

That day at Pentheus no one gets any shrift

He makes four nurses cry

For too much compassion in the Work Capability Assessments;

He disallows seven appeals against his decision to refuse disability benefits.

His employees roll their eyes, bovine, but they're scared.

Discomfort enflames his belief in his creed,

And this makes him dangerous.

Every error hardens him into his position.

No one knows the names of all the forms,

No one fully understands the system,

No one wants to be the first to admit this,

So no one is the first to admit this.

The venal mealiness of Neil's soul knows this,

so he finds himself confabulating/ Making up shit to himself to justify himself to himself.

He leaves work knowing that he has made at least twenty people's days much worse than they needed to be.

As he leaves, he is stung, badly, by a bee, and that night him and Mel argue nastily.

She turns away from him in bed

She's crying.

"Spare me," he says, testy.

----

18. Wendy is a Leader

Day five post Ivygate.

In the kitchen of the Congregational Church Social room in which the Alcoholics' Anonymous meeting takes place, Clovis is telling a story about taking his wife's ashes to her Work Capability Assessment to prove that she is not in fact capable of working, because she is, in fact, ashes.

"I say, what do you think the answer is to that, Gladys? I make the jar nod its head and shake it. They treat me like a fool I will treat them like fools in the end they chuck me and Gladys out."

YOU WHAT? says everyone.

Tiny Deb, some unfathomable age between seventeen and fifty-two, had an epileptic seizure in the waiting room at hers.

"They made me wait for three hours and I had a fit and I pissed myself right there and then and they were like oh – looks like you're using again – I'm not – we're still gonna sanction you. So I hope you don't mind but I'm eating this packet of hobnobs"

THE FUCK? says everyone.

Sylvie has brought her dog. He's not a dog to be fucked with. He's an ex-fighting dog, retired. Staffy, name Iago.

HELLO IAGO, says everyone.

There's a posh white boy, Juliano, real name Julian. He says he's "super grateful" to recovery because now he can set up his cafe. He's calling it "the Pengest Munch" Plant based foods.

Deb laughs. "You selling chicking there?"

"No, it's plant-based foods. Vegan."

"You won't be getting no visits from me then."

Says Deb, cackling bronchially, and Sylvie cackles too, a bit too long.

Double doors to the church hall swing open: *vwbf, vwbf,* like in a western.

A convenient shaft of light halos her. She strides forward and they are blinded by the light.

"Who dis?"

"What?"

"Wend?"

"Wendy you ain't been here for time, gel"

"Wendy! We thought you was dead!"

"Wendy you been getting some? You look great gel!"

Wendy shakes her head, shyly.

"Nah."

They tell her who's relapsed/who's dead/who's left/ who's done anything gossip worthy. They repeat the stories of Pentheus. They are CHATTY tonight. It's like they were waiting for Wendy to come back.

They didn't know it, but they were waiting for Wendy to come back.

In all the time she's been in recovery, Wendy has never once shared. Secretly they all think she's a bit slow. Sometimes not so secretly.

But today: "I'm Wendy and I'm an addict."

"Hi Wendy."

"When my mum died," says Wendy, "and I became a looked after child and they moved me away from here to the sea I never said nothing for four years. Not a single word. Cocooned myself in silence because it felt like if I spoke I'd fall into tiny pieces, crumble into dust."

You're not supposed to respond during sharing but at this several members of the AA respond involuntarily:

26

"Mhm mhm I feel you."

"On my forms I got them later tryna make sense of everything it says I was a bit sad after my mum died. That I was understandably a bit sad. 'Wendy seems a bit sad since her mum died.'"

"First thing I said was Wanna fuck? And I became good at that, fucking away the noises in my head. It works, for a bit, don't it."

"True."

"What I'm saying is, don't assume that you know what things feel like when you don't. That's it. Thank you."
The light dims on Wendy and she retreats back into her carapace of stomachs and defensiveness. But the light has shone.

And in the A A meeting room, over the smell of Nescafe breath, biscuit crumbs and the odours of bodies, there is a faint smell of honey.

19. The Trials of Neil Pratt

Day seven post Ivygate.
Oh Neil Oh Neil Oh Neil Oh Neil oh Pratt
You're so unused to feeling scared that
you're too scared to admit you're too scared
You're too scared of looking too absurd
But since the ivy situation, every single day
A plump bee stings you unexpectedlay
Your flat English arse so totally swollen
The pain your libido's totally stolen
And Mel looks so sad in the bed Jenner posing
Waiting for you to put your hose in
It never happens

The pain your libido has totally flattened

And you never hear the bees coming uh

Never see them stealth bees coming uh

In your Calvins in your porridge hiding

In your wireless headphones chilling, residing

Waiting to engorge and disturb you

The river of your humanity to perturb –

You are permanently sore, enflamed

But stubborn, unwilling to change

You are making worse and worse decisions

And you can't get that handsome chicken

Man out of your head no no no no no

Man you wish he was dead oh oh oh oh

Feel sure – if it wasn't so ridiculous

– that he's got something to do with the buzz.

And as if Neil has evoked him with these his own paranoiac brain twistings, Dennis is slouching, so caszjh, so handsome, against the walls of Pentheus, as Neil leaves for home on day seven post Ivygate.

Sup Brother? You look a little bit out of sorts.

Jesus. I thought I told you to stop harassing me. I'll get a Cease and Desist.

Calm yourself brother! I just wondered how you were getting on with stopping the sanctions on my friend Wendy Honeysett's benefits.

Wendy who?

Stalling for time is it bruv? Wendy Honeysett. Fat white girl. Recovering addict. Total queen. You know her. And now it's come to my attention that some of her friends are in trouble too. You know Deb, the tiny epileptic that you let piss herself in the waiting room?

Yes and like I said to you before, if you have complaints, there are correct channels.

But brother, them channels are all silted up ain't they.

What?

Lot of bees around the place, aren't there, right now. Unseasonal bees.

Really? I hadn't noticed.

Dennis stares hard at Neil's hand on his iPhone 8 ready to film this outrage and Neil finds himself replacing the phone in his pocket, flashes with a shame anger cocktail, rallies.

I'm going home.

Sure. But don't say I didn't warn you, bruv. This is me warning you for a second time. The third time won't be so – VERBAL, you get me.

Neil is about to protest, but Dennis puts a honey flavoured finger on his lips.

You got this, Neil Pratt. Wake up.

Don't worry Persephone
He will rescue you from the freeze
Don't worry Persephone
He will thaw you put you at your ease

.

20. Day Nine Post Ivy Gate

After the day nine post Ivygate AA meeting Wendy goes home. She's desperate to see Dennis but she knows she has to do something first. There's a notice of eviction on the door of her room. Section 21. Clearly Neil has actioned this. She crumples it.

29

In her ill-lit room, one bulb, flickering, she rummages into her past.

Neil and Mel have photos of themselves everywhere, family holidays, sporting achievements, ballet for Mel, rugby for Neil, uni graduation photos, lolz holidays with the gals and the boys. Mel's secret shame is the scan of the baby she lost, which is not on display but kept in her jewellery box, the most precious thing she has ever had.

Wendy has nearly nothing in her flat. What she does have is a SASSY carrier bag, bleached now at the edges but it will never ever never ever ever biodegrade, rich purple with gold writing, ambitious font. And it has all her life in it. And rescuing it from the fire was what burnt her up some more and leaves her in permanent pain, pain that she can't really even identify as it just mixes in with all the other pains, is it body or mind, she's all scar tissue and blubber anyways.

In this carrier bag are:

A plastic anklet that Hortense says was round her ankle when she found her. It says "Baby Wendy 720145"

A laminated bible card retrieved from Hortense's handbag when she died and Wendy's only souvenir of her.

It has a picture of a sunset on it and says

"He will cover you with his feathers

And under his wings will you find refuge

His faithfulness will be your shield

And your rampart" PSALMS 91:4

And under this, crumpled up tight, on thin paper, are Wendy's drawings from the night of the Aladdin sleepover, a monkey and a tiger, a parrot, a boy and a girl hand in hand, flying over the streets of London, and several improbable dinosaurs.

21. Sylvie gets ejected from Pentheus.

Day ten post Ivygate; piqued by the histamine coursing
round his body from all the bee stings,
His ego bruised from the Dennis warnings
Neil loses his shit:
Look we're not in any way idealising Sylvie
Massive pain in the arse like us all she can be
Addicts' whine when you push her buttons
dresses like a lamb but she's more like mutton
hollow face foul breath teeth missing
puckered up cat's arse lips not for kissing
she looks old, man, in her eighties
but we know she was born in the eighties
She's funny and kind and so in love with Deborah
Wants to set Neil straight about how he treated her
Neil's outraged and he's bawling her out
in front of everyone he's having a shout
Vein of anger pulsing on his temple
Neil's truly lost it he's really gone mental
Iago starts barking no one crosses his mistress
Neil strikes the dog who growls in distress
Sylvie goes batshit starts thrashing about
Barry and Stu called in to kick her out
Neil looks up to see Dennis there,
shaking his head like a teacher
you like who's disappointed in you.
And on their break, Baz turns to Stu and says,
Mate not being funny but have you noticed Neil has
suddenly become
I don't know how to say it

more of a dick/ yehman I noticed.

also, he has a new walk.

22. Dennis does what he says he will do.

Mel is pissed off.

She was supposed to be meeting Neil for dinner but he's left her a terse text

"Can't make it sorry"

And won't pick up.

In Bromley, she decides to go for Tapas alone. She doesn't want another tense evening of polite contempt pingponging between them as it has every day of the days since Vinegate.

So instead she breathes in, walks in to El Toro, orders herself a Pinot, inhales it, feels it hit the spot, sudden feeling of being bathed in honey.

"Excuse me for interrupting your evening, but you remind me of someone. You got anyone in your family called Prosymon?"

Mel giggles. The man in front of her smells of her best holidays. He is hands down the sexiest man she has ever seen.

"Pro what? Is that a name?" says Mel, lowering her voice a couple of notches, speaking slow.

"It's a name of someone I really, really, really loved," says the man, coming closer.

"Oh."

Reminiscing, Mel will swear that she had no choice

Moment of madness she had no choice

No one believes that she had no choice

But when a god wants to fuck you you have no choice

After Mel tries to find the words to describe

How the god made her feel inside

Didn't know he's a god but how he made her feel inside

Like honey is all she knows how to describe

Golden

Sweet

Delicious

Liquid

Honey.

Inside her.

Like Neil had never made her feel –

In the high thread count sheets of the Malmaison – no

In the Couples Only retreat of the Maldives – no

In City Breaks across the great capitals of Europe – no

But this street princeling makes her feel

Divine.

In the disabled toilet of a tapas bar with designs above its station,

Melanie finds ecstasy.

Afterwards they eat figs:

All that travelling she's never had a fresh one.

Filthy figs.

He shows her how.

All night they eat figs and each other and somehow they are still there at dawn. Where did the wait staff go? Where did the owner go? Where did everyone go?

Mel doesn't care.

She is filthy and throbbing and she can't walk.

She picks up her phone. Twenty-six missed calls from Neil.

Good, she says.

I've got to go, says Dennis.

I'll see you.

You will? says Mel, girlish, uncertain, trying to play it cool.

But he's gone.

———————————————

23. Wendy and Dennis Reboot

That night in Fantastic Melly's Chicken

Wendy so hungry she can't stop eating

But she's looking different – she's a fine thing

See her soul emerging from the blubber

See her joy seeping out from her

Man in the chicken shop scoping her out

Man in the chicken shop asking her out

Nah, man, says Wend.

I got business to attend

to

With this bossman,

but, you know, appreciate it.

['Don't Worry Persephone' chorus]

Are these the drawings you wanted to see?

You found them! Yes! Oh my days Wend remember?

I remember that you left me.

I had to go far away, training and shit

Ethiopia, Libya, Greece, India

Lived as a woman and a man

Gap year, I did twenty-five of them!

So you are gay, then!

Gender and sexuality ain't the same thing Wend.

34

If you say so.

Do you know what we're doing?

Do you know who I am?

It's time Wend!

You need to gather them;

Are you ready?

No! I'm not ready for shit Dennis.

Do you trust me?

I don't know.

Take my hand!

24. Wendy is so a Leader.

Day ten post Vinegate. I'm reticent – says Alison – poshest
person in the A A meeting – business woman – high
anxiety – to follow any kind of Charismatic Cult Leader.

That's 'ilarious, says Deb, you're in AA.

It ain't a cult, says Wend.

I've known Dennis for time he was my first best friend;

He just said for me to get you lot together.

But what is it?

Is it some kind of demonstration?

I'd be up for that –

Stronger together and all that;

I can make cakes.

I don't know if we'll need cakes.

I want to make cakes.

Make some fucking cakes then!

He says that Pentheus are trying to destroy our souls

A whole human soul reduced to

The magic number of fifteen points

It don't mean NOTHING it's just randomness

What's fifteen points says Alison?

hahahaha says Deb in between emphysemic coughing fits
you're too posh for benefits

Fifteen points decides if you're fucked enough to be
allowed to be disabled.

You obviously ain't, princess, says Sylvie, harshly.

Alison starts to defend herself but

Anyway – says Wendy – he says we are all godly we are
all divine

we just need to find the divine without the wine innit/
2018 edit.

Wendy suddenly becomes aware that she has been
speaking for more than thirty seconds, blushes, sits down.

Sylvie is quick in there

Riled by yesterday, she's on fire;

Whatever your mate says, I'm in, she says.

I can burn things down.

I've already done time for GBH so I'm not bothered by
that.

Anything.

I'm up for anything.

Wendy; I don't think that's what he had in mind,
think it's more of a party vibe.

Sylvie: Well tell him I'm down.

Interval.

25. Day Twelve Post Vinegate

24 August. St Dennis' day.
This is a Greek myth but we're in syncretic times
So it's appropriate.
Get with it.
It's dawn.
On Maple Road the Garage hasn't opened yet.
Safari cafe hasn't opened yet,
Bluebell hasn't opened yet,
JZ hasn't opened yet,
the Maple Tree hasn't opened yet –
and the only people around are still in last night
so they don't trust themselves to see things in the right light
If they could trust, this is what they'd say they see;
Man comes up the road – walking like a G.
He's the FMC bossman owner.
He walks towards the leopard on the wall by SR Motors.
They swear down it's like he speaks to it or something man
Or breathes on it like that Narnia lion, Aslan.
Then this giant leopard and this chicken man
Saunter off up Blean
Fucking beast of Penge for reals.
As Dennis and the leopard pass the flats of each of
Wendy's friends
The inhabitants inside them stir in their sleep;
A feeling of contentment that is so deep,
It's like for a small moment all their pain's dissolved,

Warmth in their hearts like honey and gold.
They wake,
and the feeling stays;
But there's something else as well
Focus, determination, drive –
They are all feeling incredibly alive
Like someone pipecleanered their insides
baking soda fizz
blood pumping
like their organs are communicating
like the veil's been lifted from their brains
like it's their cerebral wedding day
and their brains are going in for the kiss.
THIS is how it feels,
Feeling all of the feels,
Acuity they haven't felt for a minute,
Synapses firing like they haven't for a minute,
Something is happening,
Someone is coming;
Iago looks at Sylvie like "What's got into you?"
and she cackles like yeh, "What's got into me?"
He shakes his head, like
"Dumb bitch"
Alison leaps into her tracksuit like she's never been an alcoholic
Like she was born to do HIIT
Works out till she pukes
and feels great on it.

Someone is missing out on this great awakening

though.
Little Deb, the epileptic, doesn't wake up today.
Sometime around 3 am her body had enough
and was like, sorry, I'm out.

Dennis sorrows. He's too late for Deb.
Gods feel pain too, you know, like parents.
It's pitiful to be so powerful yet not omnipotent.
All the AA gang feel like an extension of Wendy,
So he feels like he's let down his queen.
He breaks into Deb's flat, leopard guarding
Kisses her forehead, apologises, makes a murmured
promise to her tiny body,
envelops and lifts her tiny body and takes it with him.

7 am
In Crystal Palace Park, Terrance and Merlees
are sweeping the leaves
when they see what looks like a man riding on a
Megalosaurus
With a tiny woman sleeping in front of him.
Rub their eyes, look at their secreted rum bottles
Look at each other, and back again at the Dinosaur
Swamp
It's definitely moving.
The man waves at them as he processes on the back of the
Megalosaur, and they wave back
before seeing that the Megalosaur is followed by two
Plesiosaurs and a Giant Golden Stag
Going towards the Thicket Road Entrance
and then behind them, slopeshouldered, lowslinking,

a huge leopard.

Now neither of them can look at each other.

Neither of them can mention it.

They just don't know how to process it.

They abandon their brooms,

Find themselves being called, following the leopard.

Around the procession bees buzz.

Neil, on the other hand, is vexed.
His guts are grinding

His teeth are grinding.

His head is pounding

That Little vein in his forehead popping.

If he didn't know Mel's strict views on infidelity,

He would think she'd dipped her toe in the lake of infidelity,

If that wasn't so ridiculous.

She wouldn't even know how to!

Thing is, normally when they fight he doesn't have to do anything

because she hates conflict and will always apologise first,

making up wrongdoing on her own part even if there hasn't been any,

just wanting peace, a beautiful peaceful house like an interiors magazine

smelling always of French linen candles

or delicious healthy food

or flowers.

Neil still can't understand how Mel's shit doesn't actually smell of fabric conditioner

her humanness still catches him by surprise

and this time/

he doesn't even know what has got into her

just because he had to cancel their tapas date

and she didn't even come home

she didn't even answer her phone

he feels pretty sure she went into town

he feels pretty certain he knows what went down

probably went to karaoke with her friend Carol from the gym

 – that's cool.

Paternalistic, he wants to support her letting her hair down

thinking she probably needed a night with the girls

Ignoring the physical symptoms that are trying to tell his brain that his wife

seems to have become less timid in the past few days,

ignoring the absolute certain knowledge that

Mel

has been fucking a black queer god

and is fantasising about doing it again.

At 9 am, Melanie wakes from a filthy dream

involving the man in the tapas bar

and stretches out on the sofa where she has been sleeping since the night of the tapas bar

I'm late for work, she thinks, luxuriantly

and I don't even care.

There is a note from Neil

We need to talk.

Like Hell we do, says Mel, sass like she's never had,

knowing she's going to skip work like she's never skipped work in her life,

slipping back into her filthy reveries like she was born to it
dreaming of the tapas god like she can't get enough of it
so wet she's slipslipsliding in it.

In Thornton Heath, Barry and Stu meet at Greggs for a
bacon bap before work.
You superstitious? says Ba
Nah, why? says Stu
Nah, me neither – says Ba
But I'm intuitive.
Oh yeh?
My nan was intuitive.
Stu nods, ruminatively.
Not being funny or anything, but mate,
I think something's gonna kick off today.
Stu sniffs the air.
All he can smell is Greggs.
What you sniff the air for, are you a dog?
I dunno really. I just wanted to see if I could pick anything up.

Juliano rolls off of his latest Squeeze, Perdita.
He can feel that his refractory period is going to be non
existent today
So he rolls back into Perdita
Feels so good he's right up in her.
Clovis picks up Gladys and gives her a kiss
Girl we got to fix up good today
business, business.
But little Deb?
Still dead.

42

At lunchtime, Barry and Stu notice that something is happening that has never happened in all their time working in Pentheus.

There is literally no one – no one – not a single forsaken soul – in the waiting room.

The morning has been crazy – Neil has been locked in his office and refused to see anyone – but now it's silent. The aircon buzz buzz buzzing is the only sound.

The fuck? says Barry.

I know, says Stu.

Mercy and Jacinta, the two assessors on duty, come out and stare at the empty room.

Mercy: I don't like it.

Jacinta: It's a room full of ghosts.

They stare.

They stare.

The room remains bare.

Wendy is working and crying at the same time

Dennis told her about Deb soon as he found her and she's been working since dawn

Feels like she is Deb and Deb is her

One light for each life

lost

One light for each soul lost

Doing the maths was hard

Everyone's family tree was complex

and there were rules

had to be something to do with Pentheus

some fuckrie somewhere or other
lamps of Aladdin, craft skills long lost
one for Gladys one for Deb
Seventy-two that they knew of
Seventy-two little lamps
genie lamps
genius lamps
little lights shining bright
in Penge
Souls of SE20,Penge
Lamps that represent wishes lost
not granted
And she gathers them up in her massive arms
doesn't mind the burns, the wax;
Walks out into the petrolly sunshine
blink blink
by the Pawleyene arms
standing there
holding
flames
waiting for Dennis

Buzz Buzz Buzzz
The bees of Zagreus
Don't worry Persephone we're coming for you
Don't worry Persephone we will liberate you

First one to arrive is Juliano,
Limber walking, cocky, arm around Perdita
Hey Wends, he says;

I made vegan gluten free brownies last night,

Test batch, They're superpeng.

What are we doing babe? says Perdita

It's a recovery thing.

It's a demonstration.

Wendy looks Perdita up and down.

She alright?

She's alright Wend.

She better be;

This is important.

Nice lamps, says Perdita;

I know, says Wend:

I made them myself.

By the way, fam, Deb is dead.

What? says Juliano

Check your phone.

How is she dead?

You know how

don't think she ate nothing for the last two weeks and that cough

She didn't want no help though

Sylv says she was always up asking her

Fuck says Juliano

Alison's next, she's basically bounding.

Jesus, says Wend;

Who put Duracell on your fucking overnight oats?

What? says Alison?

I heard about Deb.

I'm furious

I didn't know what to do

so I made

Polenta Cake.

I dunno what that is. Take some lamps

What happens now?

We wait.

I'm bored, babe says Perdita

Fuck off, then, bitch, says Wendy,

You ain't part of this.

Wendy!

What? Just cos you're up in her business

doesn't mean she has to be part of this.

Next up to arrive is Clovis

in a Peacocks' bag is his wife, Gladys,

in his other hand, a drum.

Something's coming, he says, gnomically,

and starts to beat his drum,

bingi, Vivian Jackson vibes,

and he ain't wrong, for round the corner comes Iago
dragging Sylvie.

She's wearing Lonsdale, looks like she's here for an EDL
scrap.

Sylvie I know you're hurting I don't want no trouble today
says Wend

I'm chill says Sylvie but there's a glint in her eye

Mischief glint

knifey

Wendy is about to admonish her with all the sternness she
got from Hortense

when around the corner comes Dennis

Astride a megalosaur, Deb's body in his arms

Flanked by plesiosaurs

followed by a leopard

followed by Merlees and Terrance

who is riding on a Huge Golden Stag

followed by everyone who hangs around the Blenheim
centre

followed by everyone who eats at FMC
followed by all the local dogs

followed by bees which keep forming shapes in the air
such as

Neil Pratt's face

and then Deb's face:

and then words in Greek and Amharic

Honestly this procession is no weirder than anyone's
trippiest hallucinations;

They're all pretty casual about it.

Feels pretty normal.

But the denizens of Penge, on the other hand, are going
batshit −

As if this was the thing they had been longing to see for
time

but never thought they would;

The carnival they wanted from the council;

Sylvie's tracksuit has lost its elastic

so she's clutching her waistband with one hand;

the other holds Iago.

Dennis winks at Wendy

He's golden, his skin is shimmering

his eyes are so green

his hoodie is unzipped
Wendy can see what looks like a sixteen pack;
glitter shimmer iridescent
she wants to run her tongue
over it
Checks herself, still not used to having them feelings.
She's handed the lamps around and Dennis hops her up
to the front of the megalosaur with him
and they process
horns honking
it's like the end of days, SE 20 style!
And Clovis is banging banging banging his drum,
bingi bingi bingi!
Someone somehow had kept some vuvuzuelas from
South Africa 2010
and they're joining in.

On the Croydon road the traffic gets confused;
The procession takes up the whole left lane.
Steady walking, drum going,
and the little lights burning.
Alison is going on about Ghandi to Sylvie.
she's not listening;
her blade is glistening.
Deb was her girl
She loved her
With her whole self.
At the road that leads off to Orchard Remand Centre
They are joined by twenty more
Cons and warders alike

Someone goes and gets ice for Deb from S and B news so she stays fresh in the heat.

Now the residents of Brookhurst Court Home for the Elderly have joined in.

Everyone helps the immobile get onto the dinosaurs. How many people can this megalosaur hold?

As they pass Selhurst park, several footballers and trainers join in.

Alison finds herself hoist up by a midfielder, she hasn't been on anyone's shoulders since an eventful Glastonbury in the early 2000s.

she's giggling like a schoolgirl

Someone's gone into Yogi News and comes out

with 148 tea lights

and they are all alight

tiny lights for all those lost souls

Alison is still going on about Ghandi to anyone who will listen, which is no one;

this is our salt tax!

this is our satyagraha!

haven't felt so present for years

Now the dancing has begun,

lead by Chantay,

Brit School Musical Theatre student,

year two,

and now they're turning into Sydenham Road,

a massive snake,

writhing and whirling.

Sylvie is crying and talking to Deb's body.

Iago has seen a fit bitch whippet,

and he's trying to mount her whilst walking along.

The air stinks of sex, death, petrol, bodies, pain and hope.
Everyone helps the immobile get onto the dinosaurs
How many people can this Megalosaur hold?

At Pentheus Barry and Stu stare into the nothing.
Something is happening. I feel it.
Says Barry.
Me too, says Stu.

The procession is now being tailed by a brand new Toyota
Aygo.
It's Mel, compelled, partly by the tiny god peanut baby
that is growing, unknown, in her womb
She's beeping her horn and waving, trying to get Dennis's
attention, but he's holding on tight to Wendy's massive waist,
holding her close.
She has never felt so alive!
Gladys rides up front with them,
So Clovis can drum his heart out.

In the News Shopper Offices, Chloe feels her moment has
arrived.
The office camera's not working but she's got her phone.
She stops writing about a minor outbreak of listeriosis and
heads out,
Catching the march as they turn into Wellesley Road,
PAPPAPAPAPAPAPAPAPA straight into her Instagram story
Is that an actual DEAD BODY?
Sylvie speaks, toothless, breathless
she looks insane
because she *is* insane

We're coming for you Pentheus she screams,
dragon-breathed, into Chloe's face.

What do you mean? asks Chloe. Tell me more.

But Sylvie gets pulled off by Alison.

You need to calm down

No I'm not calming down no more.

Deb was my girl.

At Pentheus, Neil is still locked in his office

Unaware of his impending fate

He's booking a couples retreat for him and Mel

too little, too late

Does some part of his shutdown soul acknowledge the
silence?

Can he feel it?

Hard to say. No one got this information from him.

Stu and Barry look up from their phones on which they
are both playing the Love Island game, grafting.

 – Can you hear something?

 – Yes.

 – What is it?

 – Sounds like a party.

There is so much noise,

and it's pinging off all the parked cars, refracting off the
bonnets and the mirrors,

shimmering in the heat.

The sound is deep.

The musical theatre students are in full voice.

Don't worry Persephone we will rescue you from the freeze!

Don't worry Persephone we will free you put you at your ease!

Dancing is down and dirty, tops off.

Stu and Barry hoist up their belts over their fatbellies and walk out into the sun.

In their guts they can feel the beat of Clovis'drum.

The sound is so happy and so sad all at the same time.

It's like a wailing and a keening and a cry of pain;

It's like the maddest night Stu ever had at SLVR,

It's like the most emotional he's felt ever,

Memories of 2011 riots but this is wilder,

and around the corner they come,

the unloved, the unwashed, the broken, the sick

the traumatised, the poor, the griefstricken, the thick;

addicts recovering and not so much

human beings starving for a touch

of kindness, a touch of recognition:

Outside Pentheus now they stand.

Chantay has a portable microphone,

Always ready for her big break,

And now she's passing it to Dennis.

He stands on the Megalosaur's back.

Mel is waving at him.

Dennis! Dennis! It's me!

Shut that Boojie bitch up, says Sylvie to Juliano.

Work your hipster charm on her,

Or I will knife her.

Dennis hands the microphone to Wendy.

52

What the fuck are you doing?

It's your time, queen.

Speak.

Find your voice.

I can't, man.

You have to. Do you trust me?

Wendy stands, all fifteen stone of her, on the back of the Megalosaurus.

The bass and drums still thumping

She taps the mike

Must have seen this somewhere

She's never spoke into a mike before

And this is what she says:

Sometimes you need a God to come from the east

and tear shit up

And that's what happened with Dennis.

He heard my pain calling him.

Not just my pain actually.

Shit.

So much pain, everywhere, and so much bullshit to go alongside it.

There was an urgency in me.

There was an anger in him.

We are here for all the lost souls

That you disrespected.

We are here for our friend Deb

For Clovis's wife Gladys

We are here for ourselves.

vwbf vwbf the doors of Pentheus fly open and in the sun
stands Neil Pratt.

What is this?
A moment of silence. One rogue vuvuzuela goes off.
Now Dennis is standing, his skin shining gold so shiny;
he's so fit Wendy isn't sure if she wants him to be inside
her or the other way around.

Get down, chicken man, says Neil Pratt,
before I call the police.
Why haven't you called the police?
Stu and Barry, dutty wining with Mercy and Jacinta, shrug.

and Dennis says;
You have disrespected me
I am the god of the lost souls
I am the god of the wild souls
I am the god of ecstasy
I am the god of madness
Allow me
Let me into your heart
fucker
You number cruncher, you target meeter, you coward,
you shadow fearer
you have forgot me
you are scared of your madnesses
and you have ruined my Queen
Tried to box her in
tried to minimise her
She was found in a basket; that makes her a natural leader

You have sucked out all her braggadocio
You have misunderstood
don't make us small
I am the tamer of leopards
I am the tamer of goats
I am the tamer of snakes
I am the wilder of the human heart
I am coming for you
For Penthean you
This is the tabula rasa
This is the holy terror

Animals surge towards Neil
like one super animal.
The musical theatre students are singing
Don't worry Persephone
We will thaw you put you at your ease!
Don't worry Persephone
We will rescue you from the freeze!
Neil stands there, looking suddenly tiny and terrified, in
the sun.
A sudden pang of conscience stabs him in the heart.
A sudden grief.
As he looks at the rabble in front of him
He suddenly understands.
There but for the grace of gods go I
And he kneels down in front of the rabble
Take me, he says
I have let you down
I have judged you

I have misunderstood
Take me
And do with me what you will.
Tear me limb from limb as a symbol
subjugate me, humiliate me
as I have humiliated you
Let me be an example
To all those who would follow my creed.
He bows his head, and Iago lunge-
NO obviously that's not what happens.

Neil shimmies away, snaky like always.
Standing on top of a van, he's trying to address the public.
Mel is giving Juliano a BJ in a side street;
she's lost her shit,
Living her bliss.

Wendy continues, hitting her stride.
Her voice has never sounded so strong,
she's remembering them bible words from
Hortense.
Despots don't want to hear the real truth,
But our voices will articulate the real truth
Dennis the chicken boss knows the real truth
It's wiser not to kick but to kneel, Pratt
For he is a god and you are not, Pratt
You thought your poshness gave you the right to judge, Pratt
Privilege doesn't give you the right to judge, Pratt
Wisdom gives you the right to judge, Pratt
Too caught up in the nitty gritty

To assess the shitty shitty reality you make us live and die in

The lonely grey morning our friend Deb just died in

All these lamps represent all our friends who died in

vain

But were not compliant we know we have the divine in us

It shines in us

In Dionysu

– and at that moment Wend sees Sylvie approaching Neil
with her knife, Deb wrapped in her other arm,

trackies lowriding dangerously.

She's blatant.

Just walking towards him with the knife.

Look, you, you worm, You killed the love of my life.

NO Sylv! says Wendy.

Stop Sylv! Blading someone is not sober behaviour! says Alison.

Pentheus is more than Neil Pratt! says Juliano, newly blown.

It's a whole philosophy of hatred says Clovis

We got to go deeper

We got to influence him

Make him see through our eyes

Make him dance with us

Dance dance dance

Dance dance dance

Dance dance dance

dance dance dance

and the musical theatre students are like

dance dance dance

and Alison is like

dance dance dance

and Juliano: dance dance dance

But Sylv keeps walking, shrugs off the dancers

And Chloe is papping her little heart out, can't believe she's
got this break, this is the most excitement she's ever had

Barry will later say that at this Wendy soars, almost
elegantly, through the air to intercept Sylv;

and just as her ample body covers Neil's, Sylv stabs hard

This is for Deb

This is for Iago

This is for me

This is for all of us

And Wendy falls.

Now Mel, wiping her mouth,

goes straight for Neil,

maenad screaming

You did this to these people!

These are my friends!

Fists flailing, she's pummelling him

weakly;

And at the same time Dennis cries out.

It's an earth-shattering cry of grief,

Inhuman.

It contains all the sorrows of the cosmos,

all the rage of time,

and the sound of Dennis' pain seems to galvanise Melanie,

And she takes Sylvie's knife and cuts off Neil's head,

And brandishes it,

Agave 2018 style.

I did something! she says!

Look! Look at what I did!

And then the animals come, the leopard comes, the dinosaurs come, and they trample and devour

and they quarter Neil

fragments of him all over Saffron Square

Blood bone sinew

Ligament and muscle

tendon and corpuscle

Iago and his bitch are feasting

And Mel has lost her shit,

and is face deep in his blood

Dennis is cradling Wendy, humanly sorrowing, trying not to lose it so Wendy doesn't lose it

You got this, Queen

Stay with me stay with me stay with me stay with me

stay with me Persephone

I need you Jasmine I need you.

Dennis can't you do something? You're supposed to be a god, heal her, make an earthquake or something.

Wendy smiles at Dennis weakly

Pulls out from her chest the laminated bible card which she had retrieved from Hortense's handbag.

"He will cover you with his feathers

And under his wings will you find refuge

His faithfulness will be your shield

And your rampart"

Wendy, flesh wound, gathers herself up.

She can hear Hortense, feel her all around her

sweet scent of lily of the valley

I know you don't like violence mum

But what the fuck else was we meant to do?

And now they all dance.
Mel has no idea what is happening, her sense of reality
has completely gone.
She's white girl twerking with some of the musical theatre
students, covered in Neil's blood.

And Dennis rises, calls to his leopard
who slopes off to the Pentheus building and licks it
into flames
A gentle lick sets it off, orange tongues of fire,
wild orange flames in the august sun
acrid stink of burning plastic
black smoke like ivy coiling
Someone hose Mel down!
The police are coming, the fire brigade,
we have to dance
we have to dance it out
spirit of Dionysus in our sober souls
wild and free:
godly. And they dance.

In an alternate reality, Neil Pratt, touched by the sight of
Deb, who has kept remarkably fresh in her gilet of ice
has an epiphany;
Remembering how as a child he was bullied.
Remembering how that felt, to be bullied.
How he'd resolved one day to never again show weakness,
never show his soft belly,

and set about systematically destroying the soft belly in others.

I've got it wrong, he says,
I see that now
We are all everything
We are all the darkness and the light
We are all the day and the night
We are all creature and deity
I let my fear get the better of me
Fear of the pain, fear of the reaching,
Fear of the howl, fear of the teaching
that pain can give us
He goes to Sylv: *I am so sorry about your friend*
I bear the responsibility
I cannot bring her back
But I can resolve to behave with more humanity
And I can pay for her funeral expenses
And in this reality Sylv, the scarified pain of years
of fighting melting away,
falls on Neil and cries,
I fucking loved that woman
and Neil says *hush hush hush I am so sorry*
I know I know I know I know, and there's a sudden stillness,
all the animals process around them, tamed,
The Megalosaur still carrying the old people
from Brookhurst Court
and Neil goes to Clovis and says,
I treated you with hostility
I am so sorry. Tell me about Gladys.

And Clovis tells Neil about Gladys

and Wendy realises that Hortense knew Gladys

back in the day;

they shared their Christian ways.

and everybody with a lamp to represent someone lost,

goes to Neil and tells their story, and they're all doing a
slow circle dance, ancient, showing him their lamps of loss,

And it's like all those lost people are still there with them,

The ones who lost the fight;

And Neil is crying with all the tears of twenty years of not
crying

I took a wrong turn, what happened to me

And Mel goes to him and says

it's okay baby, I will stand by you, we will work this out,

and Aftab and Ahmed arrive from FMC with chicken for
everyone,

and vegan wraps for Juliano, and everyone can see the
world, shining shimmering splend –

Until such time as you can feel, Neil,

Until such time as you can be real, Neil

Until such time as you see that we are the same

Different paths sure but the same pain

Until you open your heart and your ears

Until you acknowledge our rage and our tears

Our need to be free, divine reaching

Our need to be part of a greater something

Our need to count, to connect, to survive,

our need to grow to learn to thrive

Until you treat us with the godly humanity that is our
birthright

we will take to the streets and we will fight

we will show you all the rage of the night

we will invoke him, god of the shadow and the ecstasy

we need him to set us free

we need him to set you free

we need him to set us free

we need him to set you free

we need him to set us free.

/ends